Do The "Wrong" Things The "Right" Way...
Take
The Middle Stroll

SEAN A. FARMER

Copyright © 2025 Sean A. Farmer

All rights reserved.

ISBN:9798329294156

DEDICATION

This book is dedicated to my only child, my son, Xavier Sean Farmer, and his children—Nigel, Nyla, and Adrione.

Xavier, thank you for blessing me with three beautiful and intelligent grandchildren. When I look into their eyes, I feel a deep and uncanny connection to our ancestors. You continue to break the cycle of our family's past through your unwavering dedication to your children, your strong moral compass, and your commitment to being present in their lives.

Your tenacious work ethic and honesty are hallmarks of the Farmer legacy—traits worth honoring and instilling in the next generation. I hope this book offers you perspective and understanding, reminding you that life is meant to be lived fully, with the wisdom to know when to pause and the purpose to serve others, always doing no harm.

Zay, you inspire me my son.

CONTENTS

Foreword
Acknowledgments

1 What is the Middle Stroll?

2 The Ego and Always Wanting More

3 The Illusion of Good and Bad

4 The Middle Stroll in Your Everyday Life

5 Constant Awareness and Continuous Resetting

6 Wise Words From The Gurus

7 Conclusion

The Middle Stroll

Acknowledgments

I could write a whole second book just acknowledging the amazing family, friends, teachers and role models that, weather they see my vision, or not, support me and my art. What stands out to me the most is the rock solid, and genuine enthusiasm for my thoughts and words. While this brief and witty book will probably not make the Times Best Seller list, I feel as if the book debuted at number one. The bliss of accomplishment is stronger than any drug or drink that has ever touched my lips. Since September 2022, I have slept on their couches and in their beds. I have watched their pets and cleaned their yards and homes. They have laughed with me, and they have cried with me as it was my turn to embrace the apparent reality of loss and death. I do not believe loss of material items or even the "loss" of two big brothers, Gary and Riley, within two months of each other to be anything other than a precious gift of peace and understanding. Now, this is not the medical cannabis in me talking right now, but I promise you that death is an illusion. Since my two big brothers dropped off their bodies here on earth, the connection between us has grown and become stronger. They don't have faces, mouths, or bodies anymore, but we laugh at the same things that we laughed at before. We don't eat in restaurants together anymore, and yes, they both maintained their sense of humor in spiritual essence. No words are spoken but somehow, I bust out in laughter watching them smiling at me as I struggle through some mundane daily human effort. Their transitions, and some happenings that I won't go into have turned my belief into knowing. I Know that we are not just these bodies, I Know that life is eternal. Anyway, I'm sending the most loving and grateful thank you out to the following: Peter and Donna Ragone and family, to my entire Farmer family, to my mentors and gurus, to my amazing mother Connie, to my Rikers Island family, to my life long friends Emilio, Ray, T. Marie, Emil, Kim, Chris, Suki, Dr Joe, Thea, Chris A, Carli, Wayne P, Andrea, Val, Kobie, Jimmy, Susan, Kalief, Ali, and if I left you out I will make it up to you in person.

FOREWORD

By Dr Giuseppe Sottile Rikers Island Jail, New York City

Life behind the walls of Rikers Island is a constant collision of extremes. Every day, I encounter individuals grappling with the devastating consequences of unbridled desires, misplaced priorities, and, too often, the lack of balance in their lives. Addiction, violence, and desperation permeate the air—a potent reminder of what happens when life loses its equilibrium. Amid this chaos, Sean A. Farmer's book, The Middle Stroll, arrives like a steadying hand, offering a path that many of us—both inside and outside these walls—desperately need.

The Middle Stroll

The Middle Stroll is more than a philosophy; it is a survival tool for a society addicted to extremes. In my work, I've witnessed the price people pay when they are caught in the throes of imbalance. Some inmates have chased fleeting highs through drugs or material pursuits, while others have clung to rigid ideals that crumble under the weight of reality. Farmer's concept challenges both extremes, suggesting an alternative: a deliberate, mindful walk-through life's temptations and trials—a stroll, rather than a sprint or a stumble.

Sean's words resonate deeply in this environment because the root of so many struggles begins with a question of choice. Choices define not just the path we walk but the quality of our journey. Yet, in a world that glorifies instant gratification, relentless ambition, and binary thinking, making balanced choices can feel like swimming upstream. Farmer recognizes this tension and doesn't simply call for moderation—he redefines it, presenting the Middle Stroll as a way to honor life's complexities without losing ourselves to them.

One of the most profound aspects of this book is its acknowledgment that even seemingly "good" choices, when taken to extremes, can become harmful. In my role, I've seen people overcorrect after hitting rock bottom, throwing themselves into asceticism or religious zeal, only to find that these paths leave them unfulfilled or alienated. Farmer's framework suggests a middle ground where discernment takes precedence, allowing us to engage with life's pleasures and responsibilities without succumbing to their darker sides.

The Middle Stroll also emphasizes the importance of self-awareness, a quality I find pivotal in my practice. Farmer's encouragement of mindfulness and self-reflection is crucial for anyone seeking to navigate life with balance. Inside Rikers, I often encourage inmates to explore these tools, not only as mechanisms for rehabilitation but as foundational skills for living a meaningful life. Farmer extends this notion beyond prison walls, inviting all readers to examine their desires, fears, and motivations with curiosity rather than judgment.

This approach is particularly powerful because it removes the burden of perfection. In my experience, many people fall into despair not because they fail, but because they believe their failures define them. The Middle Stroll reframes life as a journey of learning and adjustment. It allows for missteps, teaching us that balance is not a static achievement but a dynamic process of recalibration.

Farmer's message is especially urgent in today's cultural climate, where excess is often equated with success, and social media amplifies the pressure to live extraordinary lives. These forces are not only harmful but alienating, pulling us away from authentic connection with ourselves and others. Through the Middle Stroll, Farmer gently challenges us to step away from this frenzy and rediscover the value of contentment, resilience, and compassion.

As someone who witnesses both the consequences of imbalance and the transformative power of reflection, I can confidently say that this book is an essential guide for anyone seeking to reclaim control over their life. Whether you are navigating the challenges of incarceration, grappling with addiction, or simply feeling overwhelmed by the pace of modern living, the principles outlined in The Middle Stroll offer hope and direction.

Sean A. Farmer does not promise a one-size-fits-all solution, nor does he preach from a pedestal. Instead, he invites readers into an open dialogue about what it means to live meaningfully and sustainably in a world rife with distractions. This humility and openness make The Middle Stroll not only a guide but also a companion—a book to return to whenever life feels unsteady.

For the men and women of Rikers Island, for those living on the margins of society, and for anyone yearning for a life of balance and purpose, this book is a beacon. I encourage you to read it, reflect on it, and, most importantly, to take your own

Middle Stroll. Because in the end, as Farmer so eloquently reminds us, balance is not just a destination—it is the journey itself.

Dr. Giuseppe Sotille
Psychologist
Rikers Island Jail, New York City

1 WHAT IS THE MIDDLE STROLL?

The concept of the Middle Stroll finds its roots in the ancient wisdom of Buddhism, particularly in the teaching of the middle way. While I draw inspiration from this philosophical tradition, I've tailored the Middle Stroll to resonate with my own understanding and experiences. It's important to note that while I find value in Buddhist teachings, my approach to the Middle Stroll is not strictly bound by any single religious or philosophical doctrine. Instead, I seek wisdom from a variety of traditions, integrating them into a cohesive framework that guides my perspective on life.

In Buddhism, the middle way transcends the binary thinking that often divides the world into stark opposites of good and bad. Instead, it emphasizes the interconnectedness and coexistence of these seemingly opposing forces within the whole. Consider the profound realization that both fortune and misfortune can exist simultaneously, regardless of one's material wealth or circumstances.

At its essence, the Middle Stroll encourages us to navigate life with a nuanced understanding that there is no inherent good or bad, only preferences that exist on a spectrum. This perspective challenges the rigid judgments and dualistic thinking prevalent in Western culture, inviting us to transcend ego-driven biases and respond to life's challenges with clarity and equanimity.

The Middle Stroll

While the concept of the Middle Stroll may seem simple in theory, embodying it requires ongoing self-reflection and heightened awareness of our own tendencies and behaviors. It involves recognizing areas where we may be veering off course—whether by avoiding necessary discomfort or indulging excessively in fleeting pleasures—and striving for balance in all aspects of our lives.

Moderation serves as a fundamental guiding principle along the Middle Stroll, facilitating the graceful ebb and flow of experiences without disrupting our inner harmony. It's about finding a delicate equilibrium that allows us to fully engage with life's richness while remaining grounded and centered in our being.

As we embark on the journey of the Middle Stroll, it's important to remember that it is not a destination but a way of being—a continuous process of growth and self-discovery. Stay open to exploring new perspectives, refining your approach, and deepening your understanding of balance and moderation. Embrace the lessons that life presents, whether through moments of joy or hardship, and cultivate a sense of gratitude for the ever-unfolding journey ahead.

In the chapters that follow, we'll delve deeper into the practical applications of the Middle Stroll, exploring how it can enrich every aspect of our lives and lead us to greater fulfillment and peace. We'll examine specific strategies for incorporating the Middle Stroll into our daily routines, relationships, and decision-making processes, as well as delve into the broader implications of this philosophy on society, spirituality, and personal growth. Through this exploration, we'll uncover the transformative power of the Middle Stroll and discover its potential to guide us towards a more balanced, harmonious way of life.

The Middle Stroll also asks us to confront the pervasive allure of extremes. In today's world, society often glorifies the concept of "all or nothing." We are inundated with messages that equate success with relentless hustle, happiness with endless consumption, and love with grand gestures. On the other hand, failure and loss are often painted as catastrophes to be avoided at all costs. This polarizing mindset creates an unhealthy dynamic that pulls us between overindulgence and total deprivation, leaving little room for genuine balance.

The Middle Stroll challenges this narrative by encouraging us to embrace the middle ground—not as a compromise, but as a conscious choice. It teaches us that we don't have to choose between extremes to find meaning or satisfaction. For instance, financial stability does not require relentless workaholism, nor does physical health demand deprivation or rigid dieting. By walking the Middle Stroll, we learn to find value in the small, steady steps that cultivate long-term well-being, rather than relying on extreme measures for short-term results.

The Role of Awareness in the Middle Stroll

Central to the practice of the Middle Stroll is the cultivation of awareness—a mindful presence that enables us to observe our desires, habits, and actions without judgment. Awareness acts as our compass, guiding us away from extremes and towards choices that align with our values and long-term goals. This process requires us to pause and reflect on the motivations driving our actions. Are we making a choice to satisfy an immediate craving, or are we acting in alignment with our deeper aspirations?

For example, consider the role of food in our lives. In a culture where convenience often trumps nutrition, it's easy to swing between overindulgence in fast food and restrictive dieting in response to societal pressures. The Middle Stroll invites us to approach eating with mindfulness—noticing when we're full, savoring the flavors of what we consume, and choosing meals that nourish both our bodies and our souls. This approach transforms eating from a mechanical act or a source of guilt into an experience of gratitude and connection.

The same principles can be applied to relationships, work, and leisure. Awareness allows us to recognize when we're pouring too much energy into one area of life at the expense of another, fostering a more holistic and integrated approach. It is through this intentional awareness that we begin to understand the interplay of our inner and outer worlds, enabling us to maintain equilibrium in the face of life's inevitable fluctuations.

Finding Freedom in Flexibility

Another key tenet of the Middle Stroll is flexibility. Life is unpredictable, and rigid adherence to any one path—no matter how balanced it may seem—can lead to frustration or stagnation. The Middle Stroll acknowledges the need to adapt and recalibrate as circumstances shift. This adaptability is not a weakness but a strength, allowing us to flow with life's changes rather than resisting them.

For example, consider someone who has carefully constructed a daily routine centered on health and self-care. While routine can be a powerful tool for balance, life's unpredictability might call for adjustments—a sick child, an unexpected work deadline, or an opportunity to reconnect with an old friend. The Middle Stroll teaches us to prioritize flexibility over perfection, recognizing that a single deviation does not derail the journey but rather enriches it with new experiences and perspectives.

Flexibility also extends to our self-perception. Often, we hold ourselves to unrealistic standards, expecting to embody balance perfectly at all times. The Middle Stroll encourages us to release these expectations and embrace the inevitability of missteps. Balance, after all, is not a static state but a dynamic process. Each moment provides an opportunity to course-correct, to learn, and to grow.

Walking the Middle Stroll Together

Finally, the Middle Stroll reminds us that balance is not a solitary endeavor. We are social beings, deeply interconnected with those around us. While the path may be uniquely our own, we walk it alongside others, sharing insights, offering support, and learning from one another. Relationships, when nurtured with mindfulness and compassion, become an integral part of the Middle Stroll, enriching our lives and reinforcing our commitment to balance.

This communal aspect of the Middle Stroll is especially important in a world that often prizes individualism and self-sufficiency above all else. By engaging with others—whether through shared meals, meaningful conversations, or acts of service—we not only deepen our own practice but also contribute to a culture that values connection, empathy, and mutual growth.

In the chapters ahead, we'll continue to build on these foundational principles, delving into practical strategies for embodying the Middle Stroll in every facet of life. Together, we'll explore how this philosophy can transform our approach to personal fulfillment, relationships, work, and even societal challenges. The journey may not always be easy, but with each step, we'll move closer to the balance and harmony that lie at the heart of the Middle Stroll.

2 THE EGO AND ALWAYS WANTING MORE

In delving into the intricacies of the ego, it's essential to clarify that my interpretation diverges slightly from the Freudian concept taught in introductory psychology courses. Rather, I view the ego as the embodiment of our physical self, or as my Guru eloquently puts it, the tendency to "edge god out." It's the illusion of separateness, forgetting that beneath our individuality lies a shared source—like different cars steered by the same driver.

Embracing the middle stroll requires a profound understanding and acceptance of this interconnectedness. It's recognizing that tragedies, like the passing of a beloved sports figure or a global crisis, have the power to dissolve our illusions of superiority or inferiority, compelling us to extend a helping hand with the profound realization that in doing so, we're aiding ourselves. In times of crisis, we shed the layers of ego and unite in mutual support, akin to the left hand rescuing the right from the flames, even though it receives no acknowledgment.

The allure of always wanting more is deeply ingrained in our psyche, perpetuating the belief that excess equals fulfillment. Yet, our ego, while neither inherently good nor bad, often drives this insatiable desire. In contrast, Taoism teaches the wisdom of moderation, emphasizing the satisfaction found in restraint. By savoring life's pleasures with mindfulness and restraint, we can avoid the pitfalls of overindulgence while still relishing in the richness of experience.

Our society conditions us to equate abundance with progress, perpetuating a cycle of perpetual consumption. I recall the frenzy of snowstorms in New York, where panic-stricken families hoarded essentials out of fear of scarcity. However, such behavior stems from a failure to remember our interconnectedness—a fundamental tenet of the middle stroll. Those who walk this path understand that abundance lies not in accumulation but in the recognition that we all deserve the basic necessities of life, free from panic and scarcity mentality.

As we continue our exploration of the middle stroll, let's remain vigilant in identifying and releasing the grip of our ego-driven desires, embracing instead the tranquility found in moderation and interconnectedness. Keep reading, keep reflecting, and keep strolling along the path of balance and wisdom.

Furthermore, it's important to acknowledge the role of gratitude in tempering our ego's desire for more. When we cultivate a mindset of appreciation for the abundance already present in our lives, we shift our focus from scarcity to abundance. Gratitude acts as a powerful antidote to the insatiable cravings of the ego, reminding us of the richness and blessings that surround us each day.

In addition to gratitude, mindfulness practices can serve as valuable tools in navigating the ego and its relentless pursuit of more. By cultivating awareness of our thoughts, emotions, and behaviors, we can begin to discern the underlying motivations driving our desires. Through mindfulness, we develop the capacity to observe the ego's impulses without being blindly swept away by them, allowing us to make more conscious and intentional choices in our lives.

Moreover, embracing the principle of interconnectedness reminds us of our inherent unity with all of existence. When we recognize that we are part of a vast web of life, interconnected and interdependent with every living being, our ego's cravings for more begin to lose their grip. Instead of seeking fulfillment through external possessions or achievements, we find contentment in our connection to something greater than ourselves.

As we navigate the complexities of ego and the urge for more, let us remember that the middle stroll offers us a path to liberation from the relentless pursuit of excess. By cultivating gratitude, mindfulness, and a deep sense of interconnectedness, we can transcend the limitations of the ego and find true fulfillment in the simplicity and richness of the present moment.

3 THE ILLUSION OF GOOD AND BAD

In the Western narrative, the dichotomy of good versus bad is ingrained from an early age, often symbolized by heroes in white hats and villains in black. However, this simplistic worldview belies a deeper truth: the inherent duality within all things. Much like the yin and yang symbol, where each contains a seed of its opposite, our perception of good and bad is subjective and intertwined. To grasp this concept, we must transcend our ego-driven judgments and embrace our shared humanity.

Consider the complexity of human emotions and experiences. What one person perceives as a blessing, another might see as a burden. Take, for example, the birth of a child. While it's typically celebrated as a joyous occasion, for some individuals, it may bring forth feelings of fear or uncertainty about the future. This dual nature of events illustrates that our interpretations are deeply influenced by our individual perspectives and circumstances.

Imagine a scenario where your team loses a crucial game. While it may seem like a defeat to you, for your opponent, it signifies victory. Is this not a manifestation of the dual nature of events? Inspired by Eastern philosophies, particularly Zen teachings,

I introduce what I call the "little dot theory." Within darkness lies a speck of light, and within light, a hint of darkness. Consider the example of sudden wealth – is it a boon with shadows lurking, or shadows tinged with light? Amidst the allure of riches lie potential pitfalls like strained relationships and loss of integrity.

Adopting the Middle Stroll means acknowledging the shadows within blessings and finding equilibrium amidst chaos. As the dark dot of challenges grows within the light of success, maintaining balance becomes paramount. In the tapestry of life, every event, from joyous births to debilitating strokes, carries shades of both good and bad. By recognizing this inherent duality, we liberate ourselves from the constraints of binary thinking.

Even figures like President Donald Trump, often vilified, possess facets of positivity. Embracing this non-duality empowers us to navigate life's complexities with discernment and compassion. Armed with this understanding, we can indulge in life's pleasures, like two scoops of ice cream, without judgment, knowing that enjoyment lies in moderation.

The Middle Stroll, coupled with the wisdom of Yin and Yang, offers liberation from self-judgment and opens the door to a fulfilling existence. In the forthcoming chapter, we'll explore further examples of applying the Middle Stroll in everyday life, unveiling its transformative potential in realms often overlooked.

To further delve into the intricacies of this topic, let's consider how the Middle Stroll applies in various aspects of our lives, from personal relationships to professional endeavors. By examining real-life scenarios and practical applications, we can gain a deeper understanding of how embracing non-duality can lead to greater peace and fulfillment. Through exploration and reflection, we'll uncover new insights and perspectives that expand our understanding of the interconnectedness of all things. Join me as we embark on this journey of self-discovery and liberation from the confines of binary thinking.

To fully dispel the illusion of good and bad, we must examine the stories we tell ourselves about success and failure. These narratives are often shaped by societal expectations, cultural norms, and personal experiences. However, what happens when we challenge these narratives? What if failure is not the opposite of success but a necessary step toward it? And what if success is not an endpoint but a fleeting moment within a broader journey?

Take, for instance, the experience of losing a job. From a binary perspective, this is often labeled as "bad." Yet, for many individuals, such an event serves as a catalyst for self-discovery, prompting them to pursue passions they had long set aside or explore career paths that better align with their values. In these instances, what initially appears as a setback becomes an opportunity for growth. The Middle Stroll invites us to reframe these moments, recognizing that life's perceived losses often carry the seeds of unexpected gains.

Similarly, consider the notion of success. Western culture frequently equates success with material wealth, professional achievements, or public recognition. But success, when unexamined, can come at a cost. The relentless pursuit of ambition may lead to burnout, strained relationships, or a disconnection from one's authentic self. Is such a "success" inherently good if it leaves us feeling empty or unfulfilled? The Middle Stroll challenges us to redefine success, not as the attainment of external markers, but as a state of inner harmony and alignment with our true purpose.

The Role of Context and Perspective

Context plays a significant role in shaping our judgments about good and bad. What may seem advantageous in one situation might prove detrimental in another. For instance, consider rain on a wedding day. While it might dampen the spirits of the bride and groom, it could be a blessing for a farmer whose crops desperately need water. The same event, viewed through different lenses, carries entirely different meanings.

This interplay of context and perspective underscores the importance of cultivating empathy. By acknowledging that others may perceive the same event differently, we expand our capacity for understanding and compassion. In doing so, we move closer to the essence of the Middle Stroll: navigating life with openness, humility, and an appreciation for the complexities of human experience.

Practicing Non-Duality in Relationships

One of the most profound applications of the Middle Stroll lies in our relationships with others. How often do we categorize people as "good" or "bad" based on their actions, forgetting the nuances of their humanity? This tendency to label and judge can create barriers, preventing us from truly connecting with others.

Imagine a friend who cancels plans at the last minute. Your initial reaction might be frustration, viewing their behavior as inconsiderate or selfish. However, by pausing and considering the broader context—perhaps they are overwhelmed with responsibilities or struggling with personal challenges—you begin to see the situation in a new light. This shift in perspective fosters empathy and allows for a more balanced and compassionate response.

The same principle applies to conflicts in intimate relationships. Arguments are often rooted in misunderstandings or unmet needs rather than malice. By embracing the Middle Stroll, we learn to approach disagreements with curiosity instead of judgment, seeking to understand the underlying emotions and motivations at play. This practice not only strengthens our connections but also deepens our understanding of ourselves and others.

Expanding the Middle Stroll to Societal Structures

Beyond personal relationships, the illusion of good and bad pervades societal structures, shaping how we view institutions, policies, and cultural norms. For instance, consider the justice system, often framed in terms of absolutes: innocence versus guilt, punishment versus rehabilitation. Yet, real-life cases reveal the complexity of human behavior, where motivations, circumstances, and systemic inequalities blur these distinctions.

The Middle Stroll offers a lens through which we can approach these issues with greater nuance. Instead of advocating for rigid solutions, it encourages us to seek balanced approaches that address both individual accountability and societal context. By applying non-duality to broader societal challenges, we open the door to more compassionate and effective solutions that honor the complexities of human existence.

Finding Peace in Uncertainty

At its core, the illusion of good and bad stems from a desire for certainty—a need to categorize the world into neat, predictable boxes. However, life is inherently uncertain, and this unpredictability is both its challenge and its beauty. The Middle Stroll teaches us to embrace this uncertainty, finding peace in the knowledge that life's dualities are not problems to be solved but realities to be experienced.

Consider the changing seasons. While winter may bring cold and darkness, it also carries the promise of renewal, as spring inevitably follows. Similarly, our lives are marked by cycles of growth and rest, joy and sorrow. By accepting these cycles as natural and necessary, we free ourselves from the need to control or resist them, allowing us to move through life with greater ease and grace.

The Transformative Power of the Middle Stroll

When we release the illusion of good and bad, we create space for deeper self-awareness and connection. We begin to see the world not in black and white, but in vibrant shades of gray, rich with possibilities and insights. This shift in perspective is not merely theoretical—it has the power to transform how we live, work, and relate to others.

In the chapters ahead, we will continue to explore the practical applications of the Middle Stroll, uncovering its potential to guide us through life's challenges and opportunities with balance and equanimity. By embracing non-duality, we take the first steps toward a more harmonious and fulfilling existence—one in which we are no longer bound by the constraints of binary thinking, but liberated to walk the Middle Stroll with clarity, compassion, and joy.

4 THE MIDDLE STROLL IN YOUR EVERYDAY LIFE

To truly grasp the profound impact of the Middle Stroll on our daily existence, let's embark on a detailed exploration of a typical day in the Western world. Picture the familiar scene: your alarm clock rudely interrupts your peaceful slumber, signaling the commencement of another bustling day. Rather than immediately springing out of bed, you yield to the allure of the snooze button, relishing in a few stolen moments of restorative sleep.

The Middle Stroll

As you reluctantly emerge from the warmth of your blankets, the omnipresent temptation of your smartphone beckons. Social media, emails, and notifications vie for your attention, threatening to derail your morning routine. Yet, by embracing the Middle Stroll, you can navigate this digital maze with purpose. Instead of mindlessly scrolling, you choose to engage with intentionality. Perhaps you opt to indulge in uplifting music, allowing its harmonious melodies to ground you in the present moment as you prepare for the day ahead.

As the morning progresses, you confront a trifecta of primal urges: the desire for sustenance, intimacy, and rest. These innate cravings, deeply ingrained in our human experience, often dictate our actions. However, through the lens of the Middle Stroll, we can transform these routine behaviors into moments of mindful awareness. Consider the act of eating—a mundane task elevated to a spiritual practice when approached with intentionality. By savoring each bite mindfully, we cultivate gratitude for the nourishment our bodies receive. Similarly, intimacy becomes a sacred communion of souls, transcending mere physical gratification to embody love, connection, and mutual respect.

As the day unfolds, the Middle Stroll continues to exert its influence, guiding us through the intricacies of social interaction and decision-making. In conversations with colleagues, friends, and strangers alike, we are challenged to embrace opposing viewpoints with empathy and understanding. The Middle Stroll reminds us that true wisdom lies not in dogmatic certainty, but in the humility to acknowledge the inherent complexity of human experience.

Furthermore, the Middle Stroll extends its guiding principles to our physical well-being, particularly in the realm of exercise. Whether we are elite athletes striving for peak performance or simply individuals seeking to maintain a healthy lifestyle, moderation is paramount. By recognizing the importance of rest and recovery alongside rigorous training, we honor the delicate balance between exertion and rejuvenation.

In essence, the Middle Stroll serves as a beacon of wisdom in the tumultuous seas of modern life, offering solace, guidance, and clarity in our daily endeavors. By embracing its principles, we embark on a transformative journey towards inner peace, balance, and authentic fulfillment in every facet of our existence.

As we delve deeper into the Middle Stroll, let's explore additional dimensions of its application in our everyday lives. From the intricacies of time management to the nuances of personal relationships, we'll uncover practical strategies for integrating this profound philosophy into our daily routines. Join me as we unravel the layers of complexity within ourselves and discover the profound simplicity of walking the Middle Stroll.

5 CONSTANT AWARENESS AND CONTINUOUS RESETTING

The key to practicing the Middle Stroll in a truly effective and consistent manner requires constant awareness. Our minds often dwell in a blur of past, future, and sporadic glimpses of the present moment. It's a common human experience to find ourselves lost in nostalgia or anticipation, overlooking the value of the here and now. However, numerous techniques exist to anchor ourselves firmly in the present, ranging from breath control to the resonant tolling of bells and gongs.

In the midst of any action, pausing to breathe serves as a powerful tool for decision-making. By momentarily halting our forward momentum and focusing on the present moment, we gain clarity to discern our next move. Even as we pause, our minds may wander to the past, offering insights or reminders of past experiences. Embracing these fleeting thoughts while remaining anchored in the present allows us to seamlessly integrate past, present, and future into our actions, earning admiration from peers and loved ones alike.

The practice of stopping and restarting extends far beyond the realm of smartphones. We witness its efficacy in various contexts, from children in spelling bees to athletes in the ring, and even in everyday activities like driving or shopping. Cultivating a habit of recognizing these moments and initiating pauses enables us to break free from the confines of distraction, fostering a heightened sense of presence and engagement with our surroundings. This heightened awareness is the essence of the Middle Stroll.

Yet, the true beauty of stopping lies in its counterpart: restarting. The act of resuming an activity after a pause offers a sense of renewal and refocus, akin to a refreshing cleanse for the mind. With each restart, we reclaim agency over our actions, liberated from the weight of past or future expectations. Whether we choose to continue with renewed vigor or pivot to a different task, our ability to reengage is a testament to our inner strength and balance—a hallmark of the Middle Stroll.

In essence, the practice of constant awareness, punctuated by moments of stopping and restarting, serves as a gateway to a more intentional and fulfilling existence. As we delve deeper into this practice, we'll explore additional techniques for cultivating mindfulness in our daily lives, unlocking the transformative potential of the Middle Stroll in every moment. Join me as we journey further along the path of self-discovery and empowerment, guided by the gentle rhythm of pause and renewal.

6 WISE WORDS FROM THE GURUS

LAO TZU

Lao Tzu, in his seminal work, the Tao Te Ching, delves into the relativity of concepts such as good and bad, emphasizing the interconnectedness of opposites. This perspective aligns closely with the Buddhist philosophy of the Middle Way, which advocates for a balanced approach to life, steering clear of extreme views and behaviors.

Lao Tzu on the Illusion of Good and Bad

In Chapter 2 of the Tao Te Ching, Lao Tzu reflects on the interdependence of contrasting qualities:

> "Under heaven all can see beauty as beauty only because there is ugliness. All can know good as good only because there is evil."

This passage suggests that our understanding of concepts like beauty and goodness is contingent upon their opposites. Without ugliness, beauty would be meaningless; without evil, the notion of good would be irrelevant. This dualistic perception implies that labeling something as good inherently defines what is bad, highlighting the subjective nature of these judgments.

Lao Tzu further cautions against rigid distinctions, implying that such dichotomies can lead to conflict and misunderstanding. By recognizing the fluidity between opposites, one can attain a more harmonious and enlightened state of being.

The Buddhist Middle Way

The Middle Way, as taught by the Buddha, is a path of moderation that avoids the extremes of self-indulgence and self-mortification. It is encapsulated in the Noble Eightfold Path, which guides ethical conduct, mental discipline, and the cultivation of wisdom. This approach encourages individuals to transcend binary oppositions and embrace a balanced perspective.

The Middle Way also pertains to the philosophical stance of avoiding externalism (the belief in an unchanging self) and nihilism (the belief in nothingness). Instead, it acknowledges the interdependent nature of existence, aligning with Lao Tzu's insights on the relativity of concepts.

Convergence of Taoist and Buddhist Thought

Both Lao Tzu's teachings and the Buddhist Middle Way emphasize the limitations of dualistic thinking. They encourage a holistic understanding of reality, recognizing that opposites are interrelated and that clinging to rigid distinctions can lead to suffering. By transcending these illusions, one can experience a more profound sense of peace and unity with the natural flow of life.

In essence, embracing the Middle Way and acknowledging the illusory nature of good and bad can lead to a more balanced, harmonious existence, free from the constraints of extreme judgments and behaviors.

Dr WAYNE DYER

Dr. Wayne Dyer, a renowned self-help author and motivational speaker, emphasized the profound connection between pursuing one's passions, recognizing the importance of balance, and dedicating oneself to the service of others.

Pursuing Your True Desires

Dyer believed that genuine fulfillment arises from aligning with one's true purpose. He stated, "When you are inspired by a great purpose, everything will begin to work for you." This inspiration stems from connecting deeply with one's inner self and intentions, leading to a life where perceived risks diminish as you follow your bliss—the truth within you.

Recognizing When to Pause

While advocating for the pursuit of one's desires, Dyer also highlighted the importance of mindfulness and balance. He suggested that in moments of uncertainty, one should seek clarity through meditation and conscious contact with a higher power. This practice allows individuals to receive guidance, ensuring that their actions are in harmony with their true selves and the greater good.

Serving Others as a Path to Fulfillment

Central to Dyer's philosophy was the belief that true purpose is found in service to others. He asserted, "Your purpose will only be found in service to others, and in being connected to something far greater than your body/mind/ego."   By shifting focus from self-interest to the well-being of others, individuals experience profound joy and satisfaction. Dyer used this simple mantra which he would repeat to himself over and over as a moving meditation when he found himself stressed or struggling with anxiety;

"How Can I Serve? ... Who Can I Serve?"
This act of giving fosters a deeper connection to the universe and aligns one's actions with a higher purpose.

Integrating These Principles

Dyer's teachings encourage a harmonious blend of personal ambition, mindful restraint, and altruistic service. By pursuing what truly resonates with your inner self, taking moments to reflect and ensure balance, and dedicating efforts toward uplifting others, you cultivate a life rich in meaning and fulfillment. This integrated approach not only leads to personal growth but also contributes positively to the broader community, creating a ripple effect of kindness and purpose.

In essence, Dr. Wayne Dyer's insights offer a roadmap to living authentically: follow your passions, know when to pause and reflect, and always seek opportunities to serve others. This triad forms the foundation of a life well-lived, marked by inner peace and a lasting impact on the world around you.

RAMDAS

Ramdas, the esteemed spiritual teacher, often spoke about embracing the Middle Path and recognizing the perfection inherent in imperfection. He believed that by balancing opposing forces and accepting life's inherent flaws, individuals can attain a deeper understanding of themselves and the universe.

Embracing the Middle Path

In his teachings, Ram Dass emphasized the importance of navigating between extremes to achieve inner harmony. He suggested that true spiritual growth arises from integrating both the transcendent and the mundane aspects of existence. This approach aligns with the Buddhist concept of the Middle Path, which advocates for a balanced life, steering clear of self-indulgence and self-mortification. Ram Dass articulated this balance as being "torn at every moment by the icy cold truth of the perfect indifference of God, and the bleeding heart of caring for all the suffering of all beings." He believed that maintaining this equilibrium requires one to "neither stay too high nor too low," embodying a state of equanimity amidst life's polarities.

Recognizing the Perfection in Imperfection

Ram Dass also taught that accepting imperfections is crucial for spiritual development. He recounted an experience with his guru, Neem Karoli Baba, who, upon observing him closely, remarked, "I see no imperfections." This profound statement highlighted the idea that imperfections are constructs of the mind, and in the grand tapestry of existence, everything is inherently perfect.

Furthermore, Ram Dass observed that "the world is in a state of being perfect while many imperfects continue." He acknowledged that while individuals strive for perfection, it's essential to recognize and accept the ongoing imperfections as integral parts of the human experience.

By following the Middle Path and embracing the perfection within imperfection, Ram Dass believed individuals could cultivate compassion, presence, and a deeper connection to the universe. This perspective encourages a harmonious existence, free from the tyranny of unrealistic ideals, and fosters acceptance of life's inherent unpredictability.

ALAN WATTS

Alan Watts, the renowned British philosopher, emphasized the significance of balancing seriousness with a touch of mischief to lead a fulfilling life. He believed that while structure and responsibility are essential, incorporating a playful spirit prevents rigidity and promotes authenticity. This perspective aligns with the Buddhist Middle Path, advocating for a harmonious balance between extremes.

The 7% Mischief Theory

Watts introduced the idea that a small percentage of mischief in our lives—approximately 7%—is vital for maintaining flexibility and creativity. He suggested that embracing this playful aspect allows individuals to avoid the pitfalls of excessive seriousness, leading to a more spontaneous and genuine existence. This balance between order and mischief fosters personal growth and enriches one's experience of life.

Following the Middle Path

Central to both Watts' philosophy and Buddhist teachings is the concept of the Middle Path. This approach encourages individuals to avoid the extremes of self-indulgence and self-denial, seeking a balanced and mindful way of living. By integrating structure with spontaneity, one can navigate life's challenges with equanimity and grace.

Not Taking Life Too Seriously

Watts often highlighted the importance of viewing life with a sense of humor and lightness. He believed that taking life too seriously leads to unnecessary stress and inhibits one's ability to fully experience the present moment. By adopting a playful attitude and embracing the 7% mischief theory, individuals can cultivate resilience and joy, even amidst life's uncertainties.

In essence, Alan Watts' teachings encourage a balanced approach to life, integrating responsibility with a touch of mischief, following the Middle Path, and maintaining a light-hearted perspective. This philosophy promotes well-being and allows individuals to engage with the world in a more authentic and fulfilling manner.

7 CONCLUSION

Firstly, I want to express my sincere gratitude to you for investing your time, resources, and energy into reading this book. Your commitment to exploring the concepts of the Middle Stroll reflects a genuine desire for personal growth and understanding, and for that, I commend you.

As we conclude our journey together, it's important to acknowledge that knowing the path and walking the path are often two separate endeavors. While the principles outlined in this book may resonate with you intellectually, applying them consistently in your daily life can prove challenging. I, too, am guilty of occasional lapses, moments where I become ensnared in the trappings of ego or habit. However, it's through such moments of self-awareness and reflection that we inch closer to embodying the Middle Stroll in its entirety.

Meditation, humor, and positive reinforcement are invaluable tools in our quest to walk the Middle Stroll. By cultivating a regular meditation practice, we can cultivate inner stillness and clarity, allowing us to navigate life's twists and turns with greater ease. Similarly, a good sense of humor enables us to laugh at ourselves, acknowledging our imperfections with compassion and humility. Surrounding ourselves with uplifting books, social media content, and reminders keeps us aligned with the principles of the Middle Stroll, even during moments of uncertainty or setback.

As you continue your journey beyond these pages, I encourage you to embrace the Middle Stroll wholeheartedly, recognizing that it's not about achieving perfection, but rather about striving for balance and self-awareness. Each step you take along this path brings you closer to a life of fulfillment, authenticity, and inner peace.

In closing, I extend my heartfelt gratitude once again for accompanying me on this exploration of the Middle Stroll. May you continue to walk this path with courage, curiosity, and an unwavering commitment to growth. Remember, it's okay to stumble along the way—what matters most is the willingness to rise, dust yourself off, and keep moving forward. Go forth, do some wrong, but do it with integrity, and above all, share the wisdom of the Middle Stroll with others.

With warm regards,

Sean A. Farmer

Why I Wrote This Book

As human beings navigating the complexities of modern life, especially within the context of American society, we are constantly confronted with a myriad of desires, cravings, and temptations. These temptations, ranging from the allure of excessive consumption to the seduction of instant gratification, often lead us down paths of excess and indulgence. The consequences of these indulgences are far-reaching, manifesting in various forms such as obesity, substance abuse, compulsive behaviors, and social disconnection.

In the midst of this cacophony of desires and distractions, I found myself questioning whether there existed a path that allowed us to navigate through life's pleasures and pitfalls with grace and balance. What if we could find a way to indulge in life's offerings without succumbing to their harmful consequences? This question served as the impetus for writing this book—a quest to explore the concept of the Middle Stroll and its potential to revolutionize our approach to living.

The Middle Stroll, as I came to understand it, is not merely a philosophy of moderation, but a profound paradigm shift—a reimagining of how we engage with the world around us. It challenges the prevailing dichotomies of "good" and "bad," urging us to transcend the limitations of binary thinking and embrace the inherent complexities of existence.

One of the fundamental premises of the Middle Stroll is the recognition that our actions, even those traditionally deemed "good," can benefit from moderation. In a society that often glorifies excess and equates success with accumulation, the Middle

Stroll offers a refreshing alternative—a path that values discernment over indulgence, balance over excess.

Furthermore, the Middle Stroll invites us to cultivate a deeper understanding of ourselves and our relationship to the world. Through practices such as mindfulness, meditation, and self-reflection, we gain insight into the intricate interplay of our desires, fears, and aspirations. We learn to navigate the ebb and flow of life with greater ease and resilience, finding solace in the realization that true fulfillment lies not in the pursuit of external validation or material wealth, but in the cultivation of inner peace and contentment.

In writing this book, my intention is not to provide a definitive roadmap to enlightenment, but rather to spark a conversation—to inspire readers to question the prevailing narratives of success and happiness, and to explore alternative ways of being in the world. It is my hope that through the exploration of the Middle Stroll, we can begin to chart a course towards a more balanced, compassionate, and fulfilling existence—for ourselves, for future generations, and for the world at large.

ABOUT THE AUTHOR

Sean is a retired Police Officer (2008) and a retired Social Worker (2022) and a full-time writer of both fiction and nonfictional works. He is an avid Taoist, discovering the Taoist philosophy in 2019 while working at Rikers Island Jail as a Mental Health therapist. This is his second nonfiction book, and he is currently finishing a tell all book about his ten years working as an unlicensed Social Worker at Rikers, as well as several screen and stage plays. His first book, Becoming Blue, Understanding Police Culture, is available on Amazon. He travels between New York and the rest of the country writing, loving, and serving others through the pure wisdom of the Tao Te Ching. He has one adult son, two grandsons, and one granddaughter all of whom reside in North Carolina. Sean can be reached on all platforms by using the hashtags #askanog

The Middle Stroll

#thefarmercy and #thefarmersutra

The Middle Stroll

The Middle Stroll

Made in the USA
Columbia, SC
18 March 2025